Mountains

Catherine Chambers

Heinemann Library
Chicago, Illinois

Designed by David Oakley
Illustrations by Tokay Interactive
Originated by Dot Gradations
Printed in Hong Kong/China

04 03 02 01 00
10 9 8 7 6 5 4 3 2 1

Library of Congress Cataloging-in-Publication Data

Chambers, Catherine, 1954-
  Mountains / Catherine Chambers.
    p. cm. – (Mapping earthforms)
  Includes bibliographical references (p.) and index.
  Summary: Examines the world's mountains, discussing how they were formed, what organisms live there, and how they are used by humans.
    ISBN 1-57572-525-8 (lib. bdg.)
    1. Mountains—Juvenile literature. [1. Mountains.] I. Title.

GB512.C53 2000
508.3143—dc21   99-046852

Acknowledgments
The Publishers would like to thank the following for permission to reproduce photographs: Robert Harding Picture Library, pp. 4, 20; Survival Anglia/Konrad Wothe, p. 5; G. R. Roberts, pp. 6, 21, 25; South American Pictures, p. 10; Robert Harding Picture Library/S. Harris, p. 12; Anthony King, p. 13; Ecoscene/A. Brown; p. 15; Ardea/B. Gibbons, p. 17; Bruce Coleman Collection/J. Grande, pp. 18, 19; Oxford Scientific Films/K. Su, p. 23; Still Pictures/S. Noorani, p. 24; Popperfoto, p. 26; Oxford Scientific Films/D. and M. Plage, p. 27; Oxford Scientific Films/G. Merlen, p. 29.

Cover photograph reproduced with permission of Robert Harding Picture Library.

Some words are shown in bold, **like this.** You can find out what they mean by looking in the glossary.

Contents

What is a Mountain?

A mountain is a huge, steep-sided rock formation that rises above the earth's surface. Some people think that to be called a real mountain, a hill has to rise at least 3,200 feet (1,000 meters) above sea level. Others believe that the exact height does not matter.

Many mountains occur in a long chain, or **range**. Each peak in the range is often described as a separate mountain. Mountains can lie under the oceans, rising from the sea bed. Some stick out above the ocean water. Some of the earth's highest mountains are completely underwater.

How are mountains formed?

Most mountains are made in one of three ways. One is when the **plates** of the earth's crust are pushed together or upward,

Ayer's Rock is a sandstone rock in central Australia. It is nearly 4 miles (6 kilometers) long and just over 1 mile (2 kilometers) wide. But it is only 1,141 feet (348 meters) high, so many people call it a rock, not a mountain. When the sun sets, the light turns the rock a rich red color. Ayer's Rock is a sacred place for the Aboriginal people of Australia. They call it Uluru.

making the surface rock crumple and fold. A second way is when areas of soft rock are worn away, leaving peaks or **plateaus** of harder rock sticking out. A third way is when **molten** rock from deep within the earth shoots through gaps in the earth's crust and cools into a volcanic mountain.

What do mountains look like?

Mountains give the world some of its most amazing scenery. Mountains have many different shapes, patterns, and colors. A very high mountain can be lush and green at its base, but rocky and covered with snow at its peak. We will discover more about the great variety of mountain landscapes.

Life on the mountains

Life on the mountains can be difficult, especially at higher levels. Many plants have **adapted** to the cold winds and poor soil. Animals have learned to survive in the thin air and thick snow. People have adapted, too. We will also find out what the future holds for life in the mountains.

Mountains often mark borders between countries. The Ural Mountains in this picture do not separate two countries, but they form the boundary between two continents and two very different cultures. To the west lies European Russia, and to the east lies Asian Russia.

The Mountains of the World

Where in the world?

Mountains are found all over the world, in many different environments. Occasionally, single peaks and **ridges** rise suddenly above flat ground. Some mountains are islands that seem to pop out of the sea. Many of these are underwater volcanoes.

Most mountains are part of a **range**. These ranges are often found on the edges of continents. Each one has a cluster of peaks and ridges that were all formed at the same time and in a similar way. Ranges are often separated by a high, flat **plateau**.

Groups of ranges are called a mountain system or chain. Bigger groups are known as a **belt**, or **cordillera**. The biggest belts on land are the Himalayas in central Asia, the Rockies in North America, and the Andes in South America. Longer belts can be found in the sea.

The Great Dividing Range stretches down eastern Australia. It causes rain brought by constant winds to fall on the east side. To the west lies the Great Australian Desert.

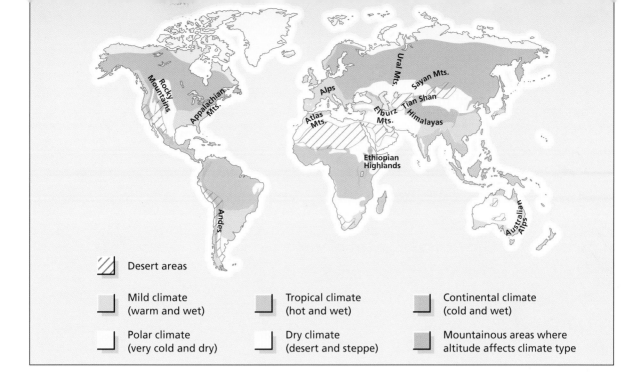

Desert areas

Mild climate
(warm and wet)

Tropical climate
(hot and wet)

Continental climate
(cold and wet)

Polar climate
(very cold and dry)

Dry climate
(desert and steppe)

Mountainous areas where
altitude affects climate type

Mountains and climates

Mountains are found in all types of **climates**, from the frozen lands of Alaska to the hot deserts of the Sahara. But mountains themselves can have a big effect on weather. The arrows on the map above show the direction of the main, constant winds. These winds blow rain clouds on to continents.

Some winds blow in one direction nearly all the time. Mountain ranges keep the rain from going further. The deserts lie in the rainshadow areas on the other side of the mountains.

When the clouds meet mountain ranges, they rise and shed their rain. But the rain rarely reaches the other side. This is why so many deserts lie on one side of a mountain range. The deserts are in rainshadow areas. Mountains shape the weather around them, too. Ranges make their own small climate zones, which affect the plants, animals, and people that live on the slopes.

How are Mountains Formed?

The moving earth

Most mountains are formed because the earth moves. The continents rest on huge pieces of the earth's crust, called **plates**. The plates move around on a layer of hot, **molten** rock. This layer is known as the **mantle**. Many mountains were formed millions of years ago, when the plates bumped together or slid apart. Mountains are still slowly rising and changing shape as the plates continue to shift. This plate movement is called **continental drift**.

This map shows the earth's moving plates. It also shows active volcanoes. Many of these volcanoes form mountains where the plates meet. There are also many earthquakes in these areas.

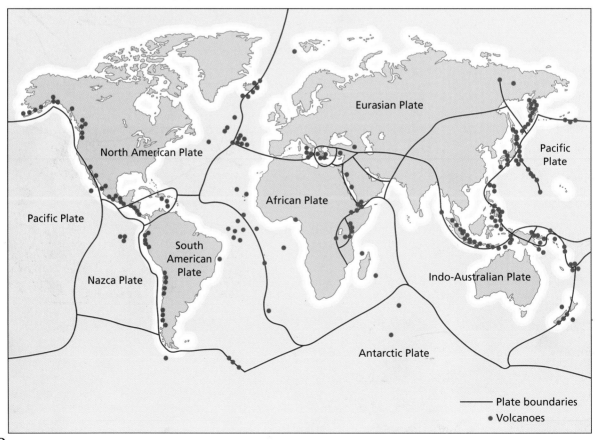

Eurasian Plate

North American Plate

Pacific Plate

Pacific Plate

African Plate

South American Plate

Nazca Plate

Indo-Australian Plate

Antarctic Plate

—— Plate boundaries
• Volcanoes

Fold mountains

Long ago, the plates jostled together and pushed the earth's crust upward. This crumpled the edges of continents and formed huge mountain **ranges,** such as the Himalayas and the Rockies.

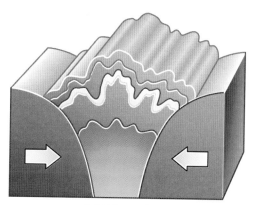

Fold Mountains

Block mountains

Movement under the earth's crust also makes cracks, called **faults,** in the rock. Blocks of rock slip up and down the faults, making some blocks rise above the others. These are known as block mountains. The Sierra Nevada range in the western United States is caused by faults.

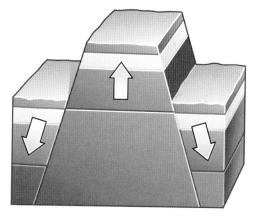

Block Mountains

Dome mountains

Dome-shaped mountains are formed when the earth's movements push up hot, melted rock called **magma** from under the ground. If the rock on the surface is too hard to crack open, the pressure causes a dome shape. The Black Hills of South Dakota are dome mountains.

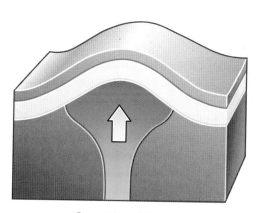

Dome Mountains

Worn mountains

Some mountains are made when soft rock is worn away by wind, rain, rivers, and **glaciers.** Harder rock above the softer rock of the **valleys** and **plateaus** remains. The Ozark Mountains in the southern United States were formed this way.

Exploding Mountains

Liquid mountains

Volcanic mountains occur where the earth's crust is thin and weak. Volcanoes can occur on land or under the ocean, where they often rise above the water as islands. Volcanoes often begin with hot gases, ash, and rocks exploding through cracks in the earth's surface, called vents. Hot **magma** rises from great chambers under the earth's crust and then oozes out through the vent. When magma reaches the air, it cools and becomes **lava**, which is thicker than magma.

The lava piles up and cools further into a cone-shaped volcano with a hole at the top called a **crater**. Sometimes lava spreads out over a wider area, making a shield-shaped volcano with gently sloping sides.

Mauna Loa is a shield volcano. It lies on the main island of Hawaii in the Pacific Ocean. The tallest mountain in the world is also a shield volcano. It is Mauna Kea, which lies on the same Hawaiian island. Only 13,792 feet (4,205 meters) of Mauna Kea is above sea level.

Some volcanoes grow into mountains very quickly, such as Mount Paricutin in Mexico. The land where it stands was a cornfield until one day in 1943 when smoke, ash, and volcanic rocks suddenly spurted out of a crack in the ground. Then burning orange lava gushed out. In one week it was a hill 490 feet (150 meters) high. Fifty years later it was 9,100 feet (2775 meters) high.

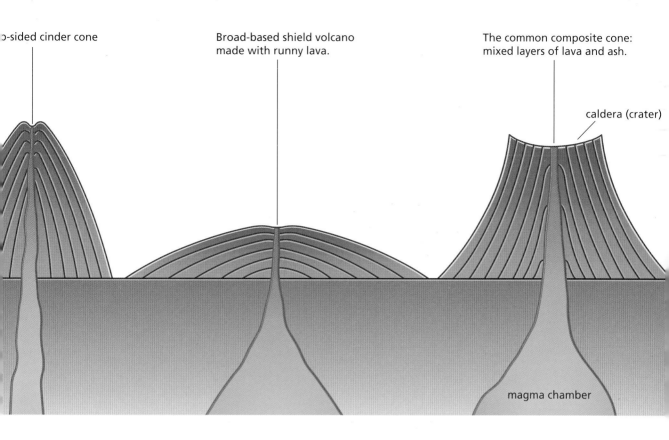

-sided cinder cone

Broad-based shield volcano made with runny lava.

The common composite cone: mixed layers of lava and ash.

caldera (crater)

magma chamber

Sleeping volcanoes

When a volcano has not erupted for millions of years, it is called extinct, or dead. But a volcano that has not erupted for thousands of years is still thought to be alive. It is called dormant, which means it is sleeping. Dormant volcanoes are very dangerous. Most have a **plug** of old, solid lava filling the crater. When the volcano finally explodes again, enormous pressure builds up against the plug. This leads to a huge eruption. Mount St. Helens in Washington was dormant for 123 years. But in 1980, magma pushed up against the solid rock. The pressure blew out a whole side of the mountain.

Volcanoes get worn down, just like any other mountain. When the soft layers of rock are **eroded** away, they leave a plug of hard, solid lava. Solid lava is often rich in **minerals**, which can make volcanic soils very **fertile.** This is why farmers are attracted to the slopes of volcanoes. Some volcanic craters fill with water and become lakes.

What Do Mountains Look Like?

Mountains can have jagged peaks or flat tops. They can be a single color or have bands of different colored rock. How a mountain looks depends on its age, the kind of rock it is made of, and how it has **eroded**.

Young mountain **ranges** have tall peaks and deep **valleys**, like the Alps in Europe. This is because erosion has not yet flattened them. Older mountains have rounder peaks and shallower valleys. The Appalachians in North America are like this.

Sun, rain, frost, and snow all wear down rocks. This is known as **weathering**. Rivers and **glaciers** carry away pieces of broken rock. These bump against the mountain,

Erosion can reveal patterned layers of different types of rock, as in the Grand Canyon in Arizona. **Igneous** rocks are made of hardened **magma**. **Sedimentary** rocks are made of bits of clay and gritty sand that were deposited by running water. **Metamorphic** rocks are smooth, such as marble, and have been heated and pressed. But not all mountains are made of layers. Some are made of just one type of rock.

wearing it away even more. This kind of erosion is known as **corrasion**. The most powerful erosive force is a river. It can cut deep **gorges** between the mountains. Frost shatters rocks into lots of jagged pieces called **scree**. These pieces are pulled down the mountain by gravity.

Mountains are not just bare rock. Streams, waterfalls, and small rivers run down them. Glaciers slip slowly toward the bottom. Small lakes fill dips that were **scoured** out by glaciers. Mountain peaks are often covered in snow, and snowsheets cover flat slopes. Lower down, plant life colors the mountain green, except where the **climate** is very dry. Then, bare rock reaches to the valley floor.

This beautiful formation is called the Enchanted City. It is made of limestone rock that has been eroded into fantastic shapes. The Enchanted City is in Spain's Sierra de Valdecabras.

Weather on the mountains

There are often clouds, rain, and snow on mountains. Warm clouds rise when they are blown up against the mountain. As the clouds rise, they cool in the chilly mountain air. This makes the **water vapor** in them turn into water droplets that fall as rain high on the mountain. The cold air also makes some of the rain fall as snow. On the other side of the mountain, the cold air sinks quickly. This can cause very strong air **currents**. These and other unusual weather features affect mountain life.

A Great Mountain Range— The Rockies

The Rocky Mountains, or Rockies, are a long **belt** of mountain **ranges** stretching along the western side of North America. These mountains were first folded upward more than 190 million years ago. They are still forming and rising. The chain has many different landscapes, from the peaks of Wyoming to the flat-topped rocks of the Grand Canyon. Most of the **erosion** has been caused by moving ice and water. The Rockies have wide **valleys scoured** out by **glaciers,** as well as deep **gorges** carved by rivers. There are long ribbon-shaped lakes

The Rocky Mountains make a **watershed** between different river systems. For example, the Colorado River flows westward from the Rockies into the Pacific Ocean. The waters of the mighty Missouri run eastward to the Mississippi River and eventually flow into the Gulf of Mexico, which opens out into the Atlantic Ocean.

and hot volcanic springs. The Great Salt Lake sits in the middle of the Rockies' widest point. The salt in the water comes from the **minerals** in the rocks around it.

The chain passes through many different **climates**, from the frozen lands of Alaska in the north to hot, sunny Mexico in the south. The Rockies also affect the climate to the west. They keep rain from reaching it, making it into a dry rainshadow area. Many rivers begin high in the Rockies, which form a division, or watershed, between different river systems.

Life in the Rockies

Very small plants grow on most of the Rockies' peaks. Further down are grasses and small shrubs. Below this lie huge forests, mainly of **conifer** trees, with grassland sloping away from them. The vegetation makes a good **habitat** for many different **species** of plants and animals.

About five million people live in the Rockies. Some people work in the mining industry. Gold, silver, copper, coal, and iron ore are found in the mountains. There is also oil and natural gas. Some people work in the forests, especially in the north. In the Colorado, Montana, and Wyoming Rockies, farmers raise large herds of cattle and sheep. Tourism also provides jobs. The Rockies have many popular ski resorts.

Rocky Mountain National Park was created in 1915. It includes many peaks, 60 of which are more than 11,480 feet (3,500 meters) high. Tourists can cross the park from east to west along Trail Ridge Road, which takes them over the Continental Divide. Deer, black bear, Rocky Mountain Bighorn sheep, elk, and coyote roam the park. Golden eagles fly overhead. The park is home to over 700 species of plants.

Mountain Plants

Growing problems

The diagram below shows different kinds of plant life in different mountain **climates**. But all mountain plants face many of the same problems. As the slope rises, the temperature cools. For every 500 feet (150 meters) of **altitude**, the temperature drops about 2° F (1° C). Plants also have to cope with rapid temperature changes, from very cold at night to hot during the day.

Mountain soils are thin and poor. Heavy rain makes any soil very wet. The soil often freezes, too. Strong winds blow, and clouds often block the sunlight that plants need for food and energy.

Mountains in the far north or south are only able to support vegetation on their lower slopes.

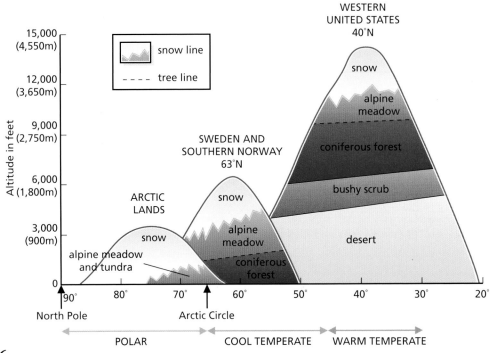

Tough plants

Mountain plants have **adapted** to the harsh conditions. High up, tiny **lichens** cling to bare rocks. Lichens are not true plants. They are a mixture of **fungi** and **algae**. Lichens are very tough and leathery. They do not need soil. Mosses are true plants, but they are also very tiny. They, too, cling and grow well in very damp conditions.

Lower down, larger plants often grow in sheltered cracks between the rocks. They flower and produce seeds in a very short time before the long, harsh winters begin. Most mountain plants have very strong, clinging roots and short stems that cannot break in the wind. Their leaves are small, flat, and covered in hairs, spikes, or spines. These leaves let in warmth and light, but are not harmed by wind and ice. The flowers are surrounded by leaves for protection. Grasses have a tough, waxy coating and are often bunched together like a bush. They sway in a rotating motion so that they do not snap when the wind blows.

Mountains often have an area of **conifer** trees. Most conifer trees are evergreen, which means that they do not lose their leaves during the winter. This enables them to use winter's weak rays of sunlight to make food. The leaves are thin and often spiky with a waxy coating. This keeps them from drying out when the tree roots are unable to get moisture from the frozen soil.

The silver fir grows in mountain forests throughout Europe, from the Pyrenees to the Alps and eastward to the Balkan Mountains. Its wood is used for making boxes and carvings. It is also made into paper. Turpentine oil is extracted from the bark and mixed into paints. Turpentine from the leaves and wood is used in medicine for both people and animals.

Mountain Animals

Mountain animals have to survive in very harsh conditions, just as the plants do. There is less oxygen for animals to breathe high in the mountains. This is because oxygen is a heavy gas that sinks. But many mountain mammals have developed large lungs and hearts to make the most of the small amount of oxygen available.

Many mammals live above the **tree line**. In the winter, some move from the peaks down to the **foothills**. Small mammals, such as alpine marmots, eat as much as they can during the summer. They store fat in their bodies and then **hibernate** in winter. The marmot hibernates in deep burrows that it fills with hay.

Mountain birds are usually large and strong, like this golden eagle. The golden eagle lives in Europe, Asia, Africa, and North America. It has to fly in very fierce winds. Golden eagles can grow up to 3 feet (1 meter) long from beak to tail, with a wingspan of 6 feet (2 meters). The eagle has very sharp eyes that help it spot its prey from very high up. Its strong talons grip small mammals to carry them away. The eagle eats meat ranging from mice to young deer. Its nest is made from sticks and twigs and is built high on rocky mountain ledges.

Many mammals have **adapted** to the cold temperatures. Large mammals, such as the yak, llama, and vicuna, often have thick, long fur. These shaggy coats trap the air warmed by the animals' bodies and keep them warm. The thick fur also protects them from the chill of the wind.

Many mammals are darkly colored. This helps them absorb the sun's warmth. Pale colors reflect more of the sun's heat and would make the animal colder. But others, such as the Arctic hare and Arctic fox, turn white in winter as **camouflage** against the snow. A white coat protects the hare from being caught by predators. It keeps the Arctic fox from being seen by its prey.

Mountain sheep, goats, and small mammals feed mostly on tough grasses and small shrubs. They can also eat **lichens** and mosses that cling to the rocks. The sheep and goats are able to climb on high, narrow ledges to find their food. The Rocky Mountain goat has soft hoof pads with hard, sharp edges. These allow it to run on hard rock or ice, as well as on soft snow.

◈ European brown bears live in the mountains. They often make their homes in caves. Long, shaggy coats protect them from the cold. In the coldest part of winter, the bears hibernate, living off the energy stored in their body fat. To keep from using too much energy, their body temperature cools, and their heartbeats slow down.

People of the Mountains

Why do people live on cold, windy mountains? Thousands of years ago, mountain caves made natural homes. The cave homes were easy to defend against enemies and wild animals. Some people still make their homes in caves. But today, cave dwellings might have modern facilities. The mountains provide materials, such as wood and rock, to build houses, too.

Many mountain homes have small windows that keep out the cold. The roofs slope over the sides of the house. This catches the snow and keeps it from piling against the walls.

◈ Transportation and communications are difficult in the mountains. Road and railroad tunnels and bridges have been made through mountains to avoid the slopes. Cable cars carry people to higher parts of the mountain.

Food on the mountains

Many animals can be found above the **tree line**. Sheep and goats provide mountain people with meat, milk, wool, and leather. Further down, farmers raise larger herds of sheep and cattle on sloping grasslands. Crops of hay are also grown there to feed the animals in the winter.

It is difficult to grow food crops on mountain slopes. Soil is often poor and gets washed away by the rain or blown away by the wind. Sometimes, it is just pulled slowly down the slope by gravity. This is known as soil creep. Farmers build flat steps, called terraces, with long walls to keep in soil and water. Terraces are found in mountain communities all over the world, from Peru to China. Many types of crops can be grown on terraces, from rice to grapes. Farmers grow an even greater variety of crops on the rich soils that cover the slopes of volcanoes.

New Zealand sheep graze high in the mountains during the summer. In the autumn, shepherds round them up and take them down to the **foothills**. Some sheep are sold, but the rest are kept in the lowlands during the winter. There is more food for them there.

A Way of Life—Tibet

Tibet is a land in central Asia. It is hidden by mountains on three sides. Most Tibetans live on a very high **plateau** between the Karakoram Mountains in the west and the Kunlun range in the north. The Himalayas are to the south. The average height of the land is about 16,000 feet (4,875 meters) above sea level.

The Tibetan people have **adapted** to the cold temperatures and thin air. They do not suffer from **altitude** sickness, which is caused by a lack of oxygen in the blood. Tibetans also use the resources in their natural environment to make a living and build their homes.

Many of Asia's most important rivers begin in the Tibetan mountains. The rivers include the Ganges, Indus, Chang, Brahmaputra, Mekong, Sutlej, and Huang-He.

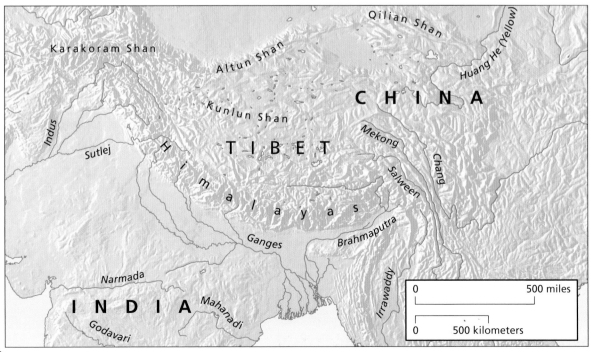

Building a home, making a living

Tibetan homes are made from mountain rock. They have thick walls and small windows to keep out the cold. Some Tibetans are nomads for at least part of the year. They travel with their herds of yaks, sheep, and goats to find the best pastures. They also raise cattle, horses, and shaggy-coated Bactrian camels.

Tibetans grow barley, wheat, rye, fruit, vegetables, and root crops, such as potatoes, on their farms. They often do their cooking outside on a stove made of stone with a wood fire below. Tsampa is a favorite dish, made of roasted barley seeds. Tibetans make wheat flour into dumplings, which are then stuffed with meat. Flour can also be made into noodles.

Some Tibetans make a living as mountain guides for tourists and climbers. They also carry the climbers' equipment. The mountains are full of **minerals** and gemstones, which Tibetans use in jewelry, but mining is not yet a big industry.

◈ The yak is a very important animal for Tibetans. Yak meat is roasted or dried to preserve it. The rich milk is made into butter, yogurt, cheese, and yak-butter tea, which can be drunk or mixed with barley tsampa. Yaks can be many colors. This is because they are often mixed, or cross-bred, with cattle.

23

Changing Mountains

Natural changes

Mountains are changing naturally all the time. The earth's **plates** are always moving apart or pushing together, making the mountains rise. Mountain blocks push up or slip down along the **faults** that lie in the earth's crust. Hot **magma** continues to force its way to the surface, adding to existing volcanoes or making new ones.

Mountains are always being **eroded,** too. This makes them continually change shape. The eroded material, such as fine soil and stones, gets swept down to the **valley** floor. Some **sediment** then gets carried away by rivers to the sea. Other sediment builds up into layers of sandstone and clay rocks when it is in the water. These rocks might one day be pushed or folded upward into new mountains, as the process begins again.

◈ Bangladesh is a low-lying country in Asia. The Brahmaputra and Ganges Rivers flow slowly through Bangladesh and into the sea. Once a year, very heavy rain falls on the mountains far away where the rivers begin their courses. This makes the rivers flood. The waters are usually welcomed, because farmers can plant rice and other crops in the flooded fields. But in recent years the waters have risen too high. This has been partly caused by cutting down too many trees in the mountains. The people of Bangladesh can do nothing about this problem, as the mountains lie in other countries.

Human changes

The mountain environment has changed a lot, especially in recent times. Mining has cut great holes into the mountains. Trees have been cut down from the forests, leaving many mountainsides bare. **Habitats** of birds and mammals have been destroyed. The soil is no longer held together by tree roots, so it slips and washes down the slopes. Rain cannot sink into the soil, so it streams down the mountains and floods the valleys.

There are also many more **avalanches**. Trees help to keep the snow from slipping, so cutting down trees has partly caused the problem. So has **acid rain**, which has killed trees in many mountain forests. Some people think avalanches are caused by global warming. Global warming is a change in **climate** that is slowly warming the earth and melting the snow. Others think avalanches are caused by too many tourists skiing down the snowy slopes.

There is a lot of eroded material on this mountain. The stones and soil are called **scree**. This has happened naturally. It has changed the shape of the slope.

25

Looking to the Future

The process of mountains being uplifted and **eroded** will never end. The forces that make and shape mountains are largely beyond human control. But people can look after the environment in the mountains and **valleys**. This will make safe, healthy homes for plants, animals, and people.

A question of gas

Global warming might be having an effect on the world's mountains. But what are the causes of global warming, and how can it be stopped? Some scientists think that flares darting from the sun are making the earth hotter. We can do nothing about that. Others blame factories and cars that burn

What is the future for people living in the Alps at Chamonix, France? Chamonix is a very popular skiing resort. Buildings have been planned with safety in mind. There are concrete avalanche barriers 20 feet (6 meters) high. However, in February 1999, 79 inches (2 meters) of snow fell in just a few days. This led to devastating avalanches. The worst avalanche hit buildings in what was thought to be a "safe" area. There are many different factors that can cause avalanches. No one really knows who is to blame.

fossil fuels and release gases, such as carbon dioxide, into the air. These gases trap the sun's heat, warming the earth. They are called greenhouse gases. Releasing fewer harmful gases will reduce this effect. It will also help solve the problem of **acid rain** that is destroying many mountain forests.

Wearing away the mountains

Another problem is that people cut down too many trees. This has led to landslides, flooded valleys, and **avalanches**. One solutions is to cut down only older, mature trees and to replant with new trees. This is happening in many parts of the world.

Tourists are another problem for mountain environments. Hikers and climbers wear away plants and soil on mountain slopes. In parts of the United States, raised wooden walkways are used to protect the soil. But as more roads are built in the mountains to reach new tourist resorts, more soil erosion and landslides occur.

Empty oxygen bottles and plastic packaging litter climbers' base camps on Mt. Everest. This kind of litter cannot dissolve or wash away. Trash is a growing problem on popular climbing peaks throughout the world.

Mountain Facts

On top of the world

The Himalayas in central Asia are home to the 20 highest peaks in the world. The next highest mountains are found in the **belts** stretching through North and South America. The list below shows the highest peaks on each continent.

Continent	Mountain (Range)	Height above sea level (feet)	(meters)
Asia	Everest (Himalayas)	29,035	8,850
South America	Aconcagua (Andes)	22,834	6,960
North America	McKinley (Rockies)	20,320	6,194
Africa	Kilimanjaro (Northern Highlands, Tanzania)	19,340	5,895
Oceania	Puncak Jaya (Pegunungan Maoke, New Guinea)	16,500	5,029
Antarctica	Vinson Massif (Ellsworth)	16,864	4,897
Europe	Mont Blanc (Alps)	15,771	4,807

Did you know that satellite pictures are used to measure the peaks of the tallest mountains? In 1999, a team of scientists used satellite equipment to discover that Mt. Everest is actually 29,035 feet (8850 meters) high, seven feet (two meters) higher than previously thought.

Beneath the waves

The longest underwater mountain range is the India and East Pacific Oceans **Cordillera**. It is over 12,000 miles (19,000 kilometers) long.

The peak of Mauna Kea, a volcanic mountain in Hawaii, rises only 13,792 feet (4,205 meters) above the water. The other 19,673 feet (5,998 meters) are under the ocean. When the two heights are combined, it makes Mauna Kea the tallest peak in the world.

Not so steep

The smallest hill in the world marked on official maps is in Brunei, in Asia. It is only 15 feet (4.5 meters) high and is part of a golf course.

Glossary

acid rain rain that has been polluted by gases from cars and factories

adapt to change to make suitable for a new use

algae simple form of plant life, ranging from a single cell to a huge seaweed

altitude height above sea level

avalanche mass of snow that slips down a mountainside

belt large group of mountain ranges (also called a cordillera)

camouflage color or pattern that makes an object blend in with its surroundings

climate rainfall, temperature, and wind that normally affect a large area

conifer tree that has cones to protect its seeds and normally keeps its spiny leaves throughout the year

continental drift movement of the earth's tectonic plates

cordillera large group of mountain ranges (also called a belt)

corrasion when stones get carried along by flowing water and bump against the river's bed and sides, causing erosion

crater hollow in the top of a volcano

current strong surge of water that flows constantly in one direction

erosion wearing away of rocks and soil by wind, water, ice, or acid

fault crack deep in the earth's crust

fertile describes rich soil in which plants grow easily

foothill any of the low hills around a mountain or mountain range

fossil fuels substances, including oil and gas, formed from the remains of plants and animals that lived millions of years ago

fungus type of simple plant, such as a mold or mushroom

glacier thick mass of ice, formed from compressed snow, that flows downhill

gorge narrow river valley with very steep sides

habitat place where a plant or animal lives or grows in nature

hibernate to sleep through the winter, using energy stored in body fat

igneous type of rock made of hardened magma

lava thick magma that has reached the air above ground and cooled

lichen not a true plant, but a mixture of a fungus and algae

magma layer of hot, melted rock beneath the hard crust of the earth

mantle layer of hot, melted rock on which the earth's crust sits

metamorphic type of rock that has been heated and compressed inside the earth's crust

mineral substance that is formed naturally in rocks and earth, such as coal, tin, or salt

molten melted by high temperatures

plate area of the earth's crust separated from other plates by deep cracks. Earthquakes, volcanic activity, and the forming of mountains take place where these plates meet.

plateau area of high, flat ground, often lying between mountains

plug solid, tube-shaped piece of volcanic rock that fills a volcano when the volcano dies or is dormant

range group of mountains formed at the same time and in a similar way

ridge long, narrow peak or range

scour to rub hard against something, wearing it away

scree small, loose stones covering a mountain slope

sediment fine soil and gravel that is carried in water

sedimentary type of rock made of layers of compressed clay and gritty sand that were once covered in water

species one of the groups used for classifying animals. The members of each species are very similar.

tree line highest part of a mountain on which trees can grow

valley scooped-out, low-lying area of land between mountains

watershed area of high ground surrounding a river's drainage basin

water vapor water that has been heated so much that it forms a gas that is held in the air. Drops of water form again when the vapor is cooled.

weathering action of weather on rock or other materials

More Books to Read

Green, Jen. *People of the Mountains.* Austin, Tex.: Raintree Steck-Vaughn, 1998.

Lovell, Scarlett, and Sue Smith. *Exploring Mountain Habitats.* Greenvale, N.Y.: Mondo Publishing, 1999.

Tesar, Jenny E. *America's Top 10 Mountains.* Woodbridge, Conn.: Blackbirch Press, Inc., 1997.

Vrbova, Zuza. *Mountains.* Mahwah, N.J.: Troll Communications, 1997.

Index